Townend

Cumbria

National Trust

HOME OF THE BROWNE FAMILY FOR OVER 400 YEARS

This remarkable farmhouse offers a captivating glimpse into the everyday life of a prosperous Lakeland farming family between the 16th and 20th centuries. Complete with its furniture, garden and nearby farm buildings, it is rooted in Westmorland tradition.

The statesmen of Troutbeck

The earliest mention of the Browne family in Troutbeck dates from the mid-15th century. They held their land by 'customary tenure', a system peculiar to the border counties which bred an unusual degree of independence. In the 19th century, Wordsworth and others romanticised the customary tenant as the 'estatesman' or 'statesman'. He owned the buildings, timber and everything on the land as if it were freehold, and could transfer the property at will. His successor paid, on admission, a fine of twice the yearly rent and a piece of silver known as a 'God's Penny'. He also had to contribute to the defence of the border, an obligation until the union of the English and Scottish crowns in 1603.

Statesmen were numerous in the Troutbeck valley. They gained a living predominantly from sheep and cattle farming, but also traded in livestock, arable crops, lime, wool and cloth, bark for the tanneries in Kendal and later charcoal to fuel the iron industry in Furness. They were proudly tenacious of their rights, and ready to defy even the authority of the Crown. Among them, the Brownes rose to prominence. Bolstered by the various professions they pursued and by the positions of authority they held, combined with judicious marriages with other families of statesmen and lesser gentry, the Brownes kept their estate intact throughout the 19th century, at a time when many other farmers in the valley saw their fortunes decline.

A scholar farmer

The last male Browne to live at Townend, George (1834–1914), was a successful sheep and dairy farmer, scholar and enthusiastic wood-carver and gardener.

He was deeply interested in his own family history as well as in traditional life in the Lake District. He carefully preserved the interior of Townend, richly embellishing the rooms with his own carvings and collections in a consciously antiquarian spirit. He also created an attractive garden, which adds to the beauty of Townend.

ROYAL AGRICULTURAL SOCIETY OF ENGLAND

FIRST PRIZE — INTERNATIONAL EXHIBITION LONDON 1879 — CLASS 183

SHEEP

Top The last George Browne in the 1870s

Above First prize won by George Browne, who took his sheep to London on the train for this competition

Left The south front of Townend today

Opposite Townend in the early 1900s

A STATESMAN'S FARMHOUSE

In many respects the house is a prime example of a Lake District statesman farmer's dwelling of the 17th century, with its lime-rendered stonework, tall cylindrical chimneys and oak mullioned windows, but like many such buildings it is the result of progressive alteration and extension. Very little of the building can be accurately dated at the moment, despite the abundance of dates on the carved interior woodwork. The plan on the inside front cover shows one viable sequence of development, but further work may reveal other possibilities.

Above The Fire House in 1948

Right This watercolour of the south front was painted by William Taylor Longmire in 1866

The oldest part of the building is believed to be the central section, constructed in the late 16th or early 17th century. It is likely to have formed part of a larger structure, though it could have consisted of a single main room (the 'Fire House' or simply the 'House') to which the Kitchen or 'Down House' may have been added, as the records suggest, shortly after the marriage of George Browne and Susannah Rawlinson in 1623. The original front door, the position of which is uncertain, would then have been replaced by one which opened on to a central entry passage (the 'hallan'), running straight through to a back door and giving access to the Fire House on the left and the Kitchen on the right.

The north wing appears to have been built later in the 17th century, to provide a new, grander staircase, a parlour (now the Library) and a 'great room' (the State Bedroom) above. This work is perhaps datable to 1672, the date carved on the state bed.

The west wing (not shown to the public) may also be 18th-century. It may be identifiable with the 'New House' mentioned in the accounts as being built in 1739, at a time when the younger Benjamin Browne was in need of extra accommodation for a growing family.

The hallan was made into a pantry with a small window in place of the old front door, and the Kitchen door then became the servants' entrance. The Dairy/Wash House at the south-east corner of the Kitchen seems to be of 19th-century construction, possibly remodelled from the buttery, which is mentioned in the early 18th-century inventories.

New fireplaces and other interior fittings were installed (as well as the Library bay window and front porch) by the last George Browne, in what proved to be the final flourishing of the Brownes at Townend.

Above Detail of the fireplace in the Main Bedroom installed by George Browne

Left The oak cupboard was built into the north wall of the Fire House in the 1670s and embellished by the last George Browne over 200 years later. The carved chair dated 1702 and initialled 'BB' for Benjamin Browne was embellished in the 19th century with the arms of the Brownes and related families – the Browne double-headed eagle, the Birkett wheat sheaves, the Braithwaite hunting horn and the Forrest lions' paws. Although statesman families were not entitled to bear arms, a number of them did, and few outsiders dared deny them the privilege

TOUR OF THE HOUSE

THE KITCHEN OR DOWN HOUSE

The Kitchen was probably built between 1623 and 1626, and incorporated a large fire-hood (a primitive kind of chimney). The Kitchen is also called the 'Down House' because it is a few steps down from the Fire House. In longhouses the Down House would have been used by cattle and needed to be lower than the 'high end' in order to keep manure away from people.

The present cast-iron range dates from the early 19th century and is overhung by a large fire-crane and adjustable pot-hooks – known locally as 'ratten-crooks'. A meat loft rises above the ceiling in front of the fireplace, equipped with rows of hooks for drying the meat. Access to the loft was at first-floor level.

The wall to the left of the fireplace is fitted up with a curious arrangement of oak cupboards, boxes, shelves and drawers, and even incorporates a longcase clock. The eight-day calendar clock is one of two in the house by William Wilson of Kendal (d. 1781).

Some of the cupboard doors and drawer fronts, decorated with carved panels of interlacing and geometrical figures, are the work of the last George Browne, who also carved the child's elbow chair for his youngest daughter, Katharine Margaret.

Slate steps at the corner of the Kitchen lead up to the old cross-passage or hallan. The narrow space on the left was once the main entrance, until it was blocked up and converted into a pantry. A short passage known as the 'mell' leads from the hallan into the Fire House.

Above The last George Browne's tobacco jar, inscribed with his name and the date 1863

Far left A child's chair initialled 'KMB' for Katharine Margaret Browne. The design incorporates leaf motifs, chevrons, diamonds and spiralled columns, and is typical of traditional Westmorland carving

Left This large glass globe, looking like a goldfish bowl, was an ingenious device for increasing candle power. When the bowl was filled with water and placed in front of a candle, it would concentrate the light on to a small area, so that embroidery or other detailed work could be carried out

Opposite The Kitchen

THE FIRE HOUSE

The Fire House, 'houseplace' or just 'house' is the name traditionally given to the main heated room on the ground floor of Lake District farmhouses. Here visitors were entertained and the family meals eaten.

Above A 'wax jack', a device for melting sealing wax (left) and a candleholder with combined tinder box, flint and striker (right)

Right A bullet-mould from the days of Benjamin Browne the High Constable

Opposite The Fire House

Originally, there would have been a peat fire, raised on a flagged hearth and covered by a large stone chimney-hood which projected into the room. This is mentioned in 1734, when Benjamin Browne records repairs to 'my chimney & hood in the house'. People could sit cosily under the hood – although the locals were accustomed to wearing a hat when sitting by the fire, as a precaution against the splashes of soot known as 'hallan-drop', which on rainy days would fall from the chimney. The Gothic chimneypiece we see today, with its carved panelling at either side, was put up in 1842–3, when the cast-iron grate was introduced – but the andirons and roasting spit remain from the earlier hearth.

Furniture
Townend is famous for its heavy and richly carved oak furniture. The immense 17th-

century table – its size was the subject of a wager in 1790 – must have been assembled in the room. This is the table or 'board' at which all the family and the servants, farm-hands and 'boarders' would take their meals in common. The table and 'two buffet forms before it' were listed in the inventory of Benjamin Browne in the 1730s.

Built into the wall on the left of the fireplace is an oak press or bread cupboard, a common feature of farmhouses in the north and often very elaborately carved. One of its uses was the storage of clap bread, the thin oat bread that was common fare in Cumbria until the 1890s. This example probably dates from the 1670s, when the room was panelled, though further improvements to the interior can be attributed to George Browne in the late 19th century.

The bookcase further to the left is almost entirely 19th-century, despite its carved date of 1687; the original design by George Browne is dated 'December 3rd 1887'. Similarly, the two fitted clock cases which stand at either side of the archway were made up by him, partly from older carved work. One of the handsome early 18th-century brass lantern clocks is signed by the maker Thomas Loftus of Thorpe Waterville, Northamptonshire; the other is unsigned and was made for use as an alarm clock.

Above Four volumes of
Dr Barrow's Sermons and
one volume on Industry,
published 1678–1700,
bought by young Ben

Below Title-page of *The
Crafty Chamber-Maid's
Garland* (Newcastle, *c.*1770).
A hilarious and rare piece
of contemporary popular
culture that tells the tale
of a chambermaid who
weds the rich farmer's son

THE LIBRARY

A unique yeoman's library

The collection of books at Townend has many layers within it and reflects the interests of successive generations in the family back to the 16th century. It includes works on topics as diverse as fiddles, farming, medicine, law and religion. We know that other Lakeland yeomen owned books, but this is almost certainly the only library of its kind to have survived.

It was brought together in the form we see today by the last George Browne. He made the bookshelves and added more books, though there were at least 400 in the house as long ago as 1750, originally stored in chests rather than on shelves, with the titles written in ink on the edge of the pages (backwards to our way of thinking). Mostly in English, many of the books were on practical and useful topics, but many others were bought for entertainment. These range from plays to locally printed chap-books: cheap popular ballads and stories aimed at ordinary people. Many of those at Townend are the only known copies.

The two most enthusiastic book buyers were the two Ben Brownes who lived here in the early 18th century. 'Young Ben' (1692–1748) was a writing master who worked in a lawyer's office in London for a while – he enjoyed embellishing his books with florid signatures. His father, 'Old Ben', bought books at auctions here in Troutbeck, and young Ben regularly sent him books from London. Books were often loaned to friends and relations, and it is obvious that many of the village folk were as keen on reading as the Brownes themselves.

Furniture

The carved oak chimneypiece, pine bookshelves, rush-bottomed chairs and other pieces of furniture date from the 19th century, and were created by the last George Browne. The pattern of the wallpaper is of the same period, but re-created in 1992, based on a fragment found in the room.

Pills and potions

Displayed on the table is a blue-and-white ceramic tile: this is a late 17th-century Delft pill slab, decorated with the arms of the Apothecaries' Company. It was used in the grinding of pills by hand and is most likely to have belonged to Christopher Browne (1703–47), a Kendal apothecary.

Top Delft pill slab

Above The carpet in this room is of special interest as it is believed to have been woven locally by a Mr William Birkett in 1768. It is a reversible double-cloth known as Scotch or Kidderminster, and made from native Herdwick wool mixed with softer wools

Left Title-page of *The Cruel Massacre of the King and Queen of France* (London, 1793)

Opposite The Library

The Staircase

At the foot of the Staircase the panelling is of 'muntin and plank' construction, an early form of tongued-and-grooved partitioning which in this case dates from the late 17th century. The stair rail and turned balusters are from the same period.

Over the Staircase is a portrait of Lena Rawes (d. 1936), daughter of Dora Jane Browne, a cousin of the last George Browne. It was painted by Arthur Crossland in 1911. A large watercolour of Townend, painted by William Taylor Longmire in 1866, hangs over the half-landing.

The mid-18th-century longcase clock by William Wilson of Kendal has a dial similar to that of the clock in the Kitchen, although this one is housed in a suitably elegant mahogany case.

Top The wash-stand is another example of the last George Browne's carving skills

Above A portrait of George Browne by Longmire, 1868

Right A spindle-fronted livery cupboard

Opposite The State Bedroom

The State Bedroom

When first constructed, this was divided into two rooms, described in 1705 as 'ye Great Roome' and 'ye Little Roome'. Later they were thrown together by the removal of a partition between the two doors, which now open into the one room.

The state bed, usually reserved for guests, carries the initials of George and Ellinor Browne and the date 1672. Their initials also appear on the cradle (1670) and a linen chest (1692). Some of the carved panels, however, are the work of the last George Browne. He was also responsible for the wash-stand, the table mirror (1881), the turned child's chairs, possibly the rococo overmantel mirror (which seems to have been adapted from an early 18th-century pier-glass), and certainly the fire surround with its coats of arms borne by muscular figures with fish-tails. A naïve portrait of the last George, painted by Longmire in 1868, can be seen by the window.

Among the finest pieces in the room are the two spindle-fronted livery cupboards, from which '[de]liveries' of food were at one time dispensed to servants. The fitted cupboard which encloses the narrow corner window contains an interesting collection of 18th- and 19th-century drinking glasses, including some with tear-drops and air-twist stems.

The woollen bed-curtains, pelmets and valances were hand-woven locally in 1985 to the pattern of previous hangings shown in an old photograph of the bed.

13

The Picture Room

This room opposite the top of the stairs is furnished as a small study, and is used to display some of the Browne family drawings, photographs and memorabilia. The contents will change from time to time.

Portraits in the room include a vignetted sepia print of the last George Browne and a group photograph, heavily tinted in oils, of his three daughters. To the right of the window is George Browne's framed collection of signatures cut from old documents, representing all the Brownes of Townend.

The Main Bedroom

This room and the adjoining room would originally have been a single large chamber, used by the master and mistress of the house. The 'clam staff and daub' partition probably dates from the first half of the 18th century, when the room acquired a plaster ceiling. Previously, it would have been open to the roof. Thus the purpose of a canopy over the bed was to protect the sleeper from the draughts, dust and occasional snow flakes which were apt to come whistling under the slates.

The bed-hangings, like those of the state bed, have again been specially woven to a pattern shown in old photographs. The bed itself is tailored to the room, as its legs are shorter on one side to compensate for the sloping floor. It is carved with the initials of George and Ellinor and the date 1686, surrounded by carved panels which can only be the handiwork of the Victorian George Browne.

The room was repapered in 1985 with a reproduction of the wallpaper which appears in early photographs. A few fragments of the old paper were found in the room, and from these it was possible to make an exact copy of both the pattern and the colouring of the original.

Top A tinted photograph of the three daughters of the last George Browne, Lucy, Clara and Katharine

Above A photograph of the last George Browne shown in the Picture Room

Left The dressing table in the Main Bedroom

Opposite The Main Bedroom

15

The Small Bedroom

The bed, dated 1684, once again has the initials of George and Ellinor, who also apparently put up the fitted clothes press of 1672 to the left of the door. The linen closet nearby is probably the one that Benjamin Browne described in 1731 as 'ye Clossett over my Entery into ye House'.

At the opposite end of the room is a panelled closet, with the date 1670 and some inserted armorial panels of the 19th century. The silk brocade wedding dress on display is that of Lucy Walker, who married George Browne (1804–48) in 1832.

The Servants' Rooms

The bedrooms used latterly by the housekeeper and maidservants are accessible from the Kitchen by an early 17th-century spiral staircase made from solid blocks of oak. The timber-framed partitions are again 18th-century. Although the housekeeper's elm bedstead was installed by the Brownes, the two smaller beds have been acquired

more recently, along with the bedding.

The standard of furnishing and decoration in these rooms is plainer than in the family's rooms, but the servants were none the less provided with their own washing facilities. The housekeeper also had a wall clock – albeit a cheap American model. Clocks of this type were mass-produced in the 1840s by Chauncey Jerome of New Haven, Connecticut: they all had a rectangular dial mounted in an ogee-section (convex) portrait frame – hence the manufacturer's description of it as 'the O.G. clock for everyone'.

The wallpaper in the housekeeper's room was hung in 1990. It is a reproduction of a machine-printed paper of *c.*1900, a fragment of which was discovered behind the clock in 1987, when the clock was taken down for repair.

Return down the oak spiral stairs to the Kitchen. A short flight of steps from the Kitchen entrance leads down to the Dairy, now equipped as a wash-house, but probably the room described in the early 18th century as 'the Buttery'.

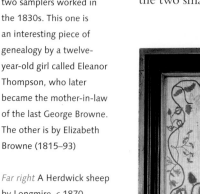

Right On the walls of the Small Bedroom are two samplers worked in the 1830s. This one is an interesting piece of genealogy by a twelve-year-old girl called Eleanor Thompson, who later became the mother-in-law of the last George Browne. The other is by Elizabeth Browne (1815–93)

Far right A Herdwick sheep by Longmire, *c.*1870, on display in the Small Bedroom. The last George Browne made the oak frame

Top Lucy Walker's wedding
dress, 1832

Left Three chests in
the Servants' Rooms were
converted into wardrobes
by standing them on end.
The two dated 1666 may
be the 'Two Meal Chests'
which were in the 'Low
Loft' in about 1731

THE GARDEN

RE-CREATING THE VISION OF ONE MAN AND HIS GARDEN

The English cottage-style garden is a partial re-creation of the last George Browne's garden. George made many notes about his garden, recording successes and failures, planting schemes and lists – he even jotted down a list of 'troublesome weeds', including 'Willarherb' (Rose bay willow herb) and Enchanters Nightshade. George's notes, together with his orders of seeds, cuttings and surviving garden plans (including a 'Roses Map' of 1902) give ample evidence of how his garden must have looked and form the basis of the current garden design.

Opposite **The garden in summer with George Browne's (1741–1804) sundial at the centre**

Below **Townend farmhouse and garden**

Content and colour

George Browne clearly had a passion for flowers and planted many varieties. His favourites included phloxes (he planted 28 varieties in 1909, all in alphabetical order), delphiniums, sweet-peas (nineteen varieties were planted one year) and pansies, for which he won a number of prizes. The garden must have been a riot of colour and was obviously well-known, as George records how people brought him plants and seeds to try.

George also grew vegetables and herbs, which he cultivated in a cold frame. In addition, he was responsible for establishing an orchard at Townend. This included varieties of apples such as 'Golden Pippins' and 'Sarah Brown', as well as plums, damsons and greengages. Similarly to today's gardener, George was troubled with weeds and pests, noting that the snails were a problem again.

The brass sundial, mounted on a stone shaft in the centre of the garden, was made for George Browne (1741–1804) and is dated 1766. It was moved and reused by Victorian George on the plan we see today. The handsome yew trees are recorded as being planted in 1736 by Tommy Benson and his son at the request of the Brownes, for the sum of two shillings.

Top Old Ben's diary for 1731, written in an almanac, with palmistry card on the left, and a list of books loaned to neighbours on the right

Above Margaret Browne (1842–1909), who married the last George Browne. This photograph is displayed in the Library

Opposite Signatures of the Brownes of Townend, collated by the last George Browne

At home at Townend

The first Browne of Townend of whom there is any record is George Browne, yeoman, who lived there in 1525. He was a man of substance, possessing four tenements in Troutbeck and a mill at Limefitt, higher up the valley. It is likely that his family had been established at Townend since at least the mid-15th century.

In 1623 the great-grandson of the first George Browne, another George (1596–1685), married Susannah Rawlinson of Grizedale Hall in High Furness. The match raised him up the social ladder, and their marriage settlement stipulated that he should carry out much new building at Townend. His son, yet another George (1626–1703), was styled 'gentleman' rather than 'yeoman', and married Ellinor Fearon, who was descended from the respectable Fletchers of Moresby and the Senhouses of Netherhall, both in Cumberland. In 1667 this George was appointed High Constable of Kendal Ward (ie south Westmorland).

The High Constable's son, Benjamin Browne (1664–1748), held the same office between 1711 and 1732, and had to call the train-bands (local militia) to arms in 1715 when James Stuart (the 'Old Pretender') invaded from north of the border.

In the 18th century, members of the Browne family were to be found in a variety of professions. George, the eldest son of Benjamin Browne, became Clerk to the Board of Works at Berwick Docks. The youngest son, Christopher, practised as an apothecary in Kendal, becoming Mayor of the town in 1735. Benjamin (1692–1748), the second son, trained as a lawyer in London. He inherited Townend, but died shortly before his father, leaving a seven-year-old son, George.

The last Brownes at Townend

This George Browne (1741–1804) became a solicitor. He had a large family, of whom one son became a doctor at Ambleside, another became Vicar of Carlton in Cleveland, while a grandson became Bishop of Bristol. The Townend estates passed to the eldest son, George (1779–1838), then to his eldest son, another George (1804–48), and so to the last George Browne (1834–1914).

The preservation of Townend and its contents, including the family's records, owes much to the last George Browne, who was a noted antiquary. As his obituary in the *Westmorland Gazette* stated, 'He has long been an authority on the tenure of the property in this part of the country… He had a wonderful memory, and was always ready to give of his knowledge. Being possessed with a fund of dry humour he was fond of a "crack" and would tell of happenings 60 or 70 years ago'.

On George's death in 1914 Townend was left to his surviving daughter, Clara Jane, who died in 1943. The property was bequeathed to a cousin, Richard Browne, who in 1944 sold it to Oswald Hedley.

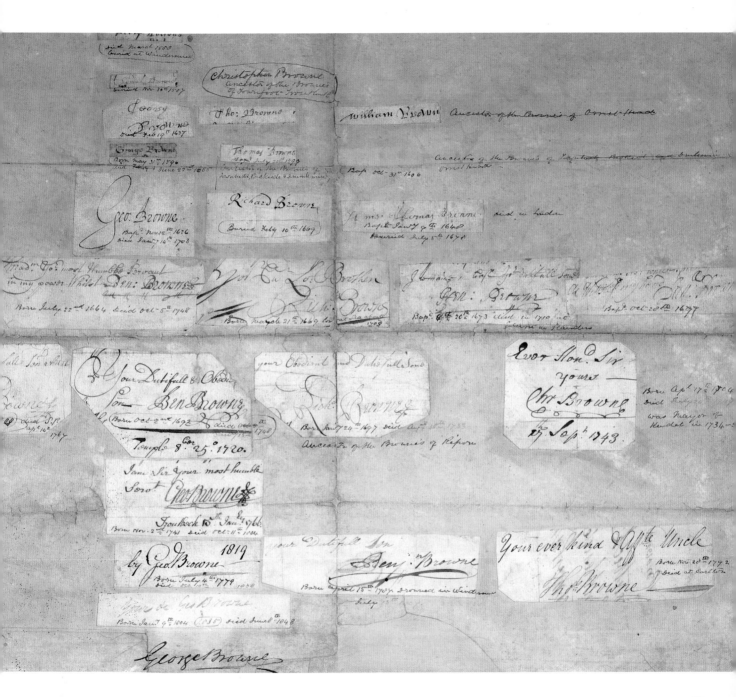

Townend comes to the National Trust

When Hedley died in 1945, Townend and Townend Farm with its fine 17th-century barn were accepted by the Treasury in satisfaction of Estate Duty and transferred to the National Trust in 1948. At the same time the Trust bought the contents of the house. The estate extends to 324 hectares (801 acres), consisting of the nearby fields with an 'allotment' of heathland running up to Wansfell Pike and a larger allotment extending from Kirkstone Pass to the boundary of Troutbeck Park (another Trust property), at the head of the valley. Members of the wider Browne family, now scattered worldwide, still take a keen interest in Townend.

Looking after Townend

The National Trust staff, volunteers and tenants continue to care for Townend, its farmland and collection of furniture. During the open season, we clean the house every morning and closely monitor the temperature and relative humidity in order to minimise the impact of 25,000 visitors on the building and its contents. We have to close the property during the winter to allow for thorough cleaning and repair work to take place. This could include refreshing the decoration or bringing in specialist conservators to works on books, ceramics, paintings and other objects, with the intention of preserving the house for visitors to enjoy for the next 400 years and beyond. The beauty of Townend is that changes are small and reflect the antiquarian spirit of the last George Browne and his love of the place.

Left Looking up towards Kirkstone Pass from the south

Opposite The National Trust gratefully acknowledges the dedication of Margaret Gregg, who cared for Townend for 40 years until her death on 1 April 2004. This portrait was painted in 1989 by Ian Cowell

Pedigree of the Brownes of Townend

(Owners of Townend are set in **bold** type)

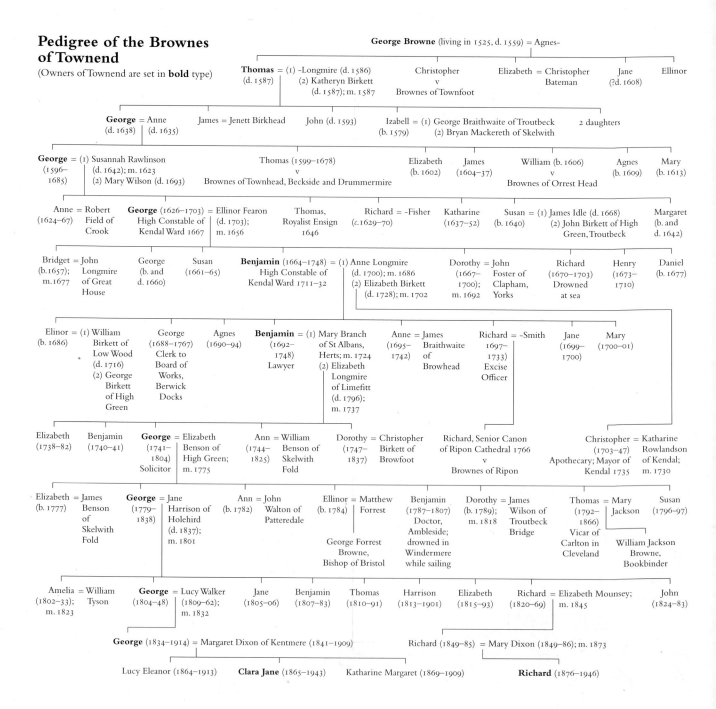

George Browne (living in 1525, d. 1559) = Agnes-

Thomas = (1) -Longmire (d. 1586) | Christopher | Elizabeth = Christopher Bateman | Jane (?d. 1608) | Ellinor
(d. 1587) (2) Katheryn Birkett (d. 1587); m. 1587 | v Brownes of Townfoot

George = Anne (d. 1638) (d. 1635) | James = Jenett Birkhead | John (d. 1593) | Izabell = (1) George Braithwaite of Troutbeck (b. 1579) (2) Bryan Mackereth of Skelwith | 2 daughters

George (1596–1685) = (1) Susannah Rawlinson (d. 1642); m. 1623 (2) Mary Wilson (d. 1693) | Thomas (1599–1678) v Brownes of Townhead, Beckside and Drummermire | Elizabeth (b. 1602) | James (1604–37) | William (b. 1606) v Brownes of Orrest Head | Agnes (b. 1609) | Mary (b. 1613)

Anne (1624–67) = Robert Field of Crook | **George** (1626–1703) High Constable of Kendal Ward 1667 = Ellinor Fearon (d. 1703); m. 1656 | Thomas, Royalist Ensign 1646 | Richard = -Fisher (c.1629–70) | Katharine (1637–52) | Susan (b. 1640) = (1) James Idle (d. 1668) (2) John Birkett of High Green, Troutbeck | Margaret (b. and d. 1642)

Bridget (b.1657); m.1677 = John Longmire of Great House | George (b. and d. 1660) | Susan (1661–65) | **Benjamin** (1664–1748) High Constable of Kendal Ward 1711–32 = (1) Anne Longmire (d. 1700); m. 1686 (2) Elizabeth Birkett (d. 1728); m. 1702 | Dorothy (1667–1700); m. 1692 = John Foster of Clapham, Yorks | Richard (1670–1703) Drowned at sea | Henry (1673–1710) | Daniel (b. 1677)

Elinor (b. 1686) = (1) William Birkett of Low Wood (d. 1716) (2) George Birkett of High Green | George (1688–1767) Clerk to Board of Works, Berwick Docks | Agnes (1690–94) | **Benjamin** (1692–1748) Lawyer = (1) Mary Branch of St Albans, Herts; m. 1724 (2) Elizabeth Longmire of Limefitt (d. 1796); m. 1737 | Anne (1695–1742) = James Braithwaite of Browhead | Richard (1697–1733) = -Smith Excise Officer | Jane (1699–1700) | Mary (1700–01)

Elizabeth (1738–82) | Benjamin (1740–41) | **George** (1741–1804) Solicitor = Elizabeth Benson of High Green; m. 1775 | Ann (1744–1825) = William Benson of Skelwith Fold | Dorothy (1747–1837) = Christopher Birkett of Browfoot | Richard, Senior Canon of Ripon Cathedral 1766 v Brownes of Ripon | Christopher (1703–47) Apothecary; Mayor of Kendal 1735 = Katharine Rowlandson of Kendal; m. 1730

Elizabeth (b. 1777) = James Benson of Skelwith Fold | **George** (1779–1838) = Jane Harrison of Holehird (d. 1837); m. 1801 | Ann (b. 1782) = John Walton of Patteredale | Ellinor (b. 1784) = Matthew Forrest | George Forrest Browne, Bishop of Bristol | Benjamin (1787–1807) Doctor, Ambleside; drowned in Windermere while sailing | Dorothy (b. 1789); m. 1818 = James Wilson of Troutbeck Bridge | Thomas (1792–1866) Vicar of Carlton in Cleveland = Mary Jackson | William Jackson Browne, Bookbinder | Susan (1796–97)

Amelia (1802–33); m. 1823 = William Tyson | **George** (1804–48) = Lucy Walker (1809–62); m. 1832 | Jane (1805–06) | Benjamin (1807–83) | Thomas (1810–91) | Harrison (1813–1901) | Elizabeth (1815–93) | Richard (1820–69) = Elizabeth Mounsey; m. 1845 | John (1824–83)

George (1834–1914) = Margaret Dixon of Kentmere (1841–1909) | Richard (1849–85) = Mary Dixon (1849–86); m. 1873

Lucy Eleanor (1864–1913) | **Clara Jane** (1865–1943) | Katharine Margaret (1869–1909) | **Richard** (1876–1946)